SUZANNE BYRD

ADHD and Girls

An introductory guide: from symptoms to support.

MENTAL
HEALTH
PUBLISHING

CELEBRATING DIVERSITY

First published by Mental Health Publishing 2020

First edition

Editing by Pinky Hashmi
Cover art by Billy Joe

This book was professionally typeset on Reedsy.
Find out more at reedsy.com

Contents

Mental Health Publishing

We're a small imprint based in England and at the heart of our mission is to celebrate the diversity of mental wellbeing all across the globe. Previous books in this series on ADHD Insights have covered ADHD and Women; Managing Relationships with ADHD and also Getting Organised with ADHD. You can find out more about these books as well as our organisation on MentalHealthPublishing.com

Follow us on the below social media sites:

Twitter: https://twitter.com/mentalhealthpu1

Pinterest: https://www.pinterest.co.uk/mentalhealthpublishing

Introduction

I have recently published a book called ADHD and women in which I talked about the salient points of ADHD when it comes to gender differences. this book has proven to be very popular and the reason for this is that women are under diagnosed when it comes to the neuro-developmental disorder of ADHD[1].

In a similar vein I also wanted to write a book about ADHD and girls, so that the particular signs and symptoms which affect girls can be better understood. The under-diagnosis actually begins when someone is a child, and through a combination of low index of clinical suspicion, different symptoms and the development of coping strategies in girls that mask their ADHD better than boys, ADHD in girls continues to be under reported. What is particularly worrying is that the literature suggest, "If not properly diagnosed and treated, girls with ADHD experience the same negative consequences as boys, including poor academic performance and behavioural problems."[2].

According to the Centres for Disease Control (CDC), in 2016

---

[1] See the article here: https://www.ncbi.nlm.nih.gov/pmc/articles/PMC4195638/

[2] ibid.

12.9 percent of 5 to 17 year-old boys were diagnosed with ADHD, whilst only 5.6 percent of 5 to 17-year-old girls.[3] To put it simply, boys are more than twice as likely as girls to obtain a diagnosis of ADHD.

This has actually brought about a mistaken belief amongst many that ADHD is a 'boys' problem' that seldom affects girls, whereas in actual fact the issue is a complete lack of understanding of the coping strategies employed by girls one the one hand (in part due to the different socialisation they undergo in society), and a lack of appreciation of the internally focused signs and symptoms displayed by girls, on the other. In popular literature it is the *hyperactivity* symptom of ADHD that is giving the most air time and the inattentiveness dimension is not really focused on (which happens to be the type of ADHD most affecting girls.

A little side note must be mentioned, then, at this stage where i briefly discuss the three main subtypes of ADHD:

1) Mainly **hyperactivity**-related signs and symptoms

2) Mainly **inattentiveness**-related signs and symptoms

3) A **combination** of both hyperactivity and inattentiveness signs and symptoms

The fact that there are three sub-types is a fact that is little appreciated amongst popular discourse on the subject, and the related fact that inattentiveness by its definition is a less obvious sign than hyperactivity does make it harder to detect. When you

---

[3] For more information see: https://www.cdc.gov/ncbddd/adhd/data.html

then add in the fact that girls and women are more likely to suffer from the inattentive subtype of ADHD, you can see why there is under reporting and under diagnosis of ADHD in girls. This, however, doesn't tell you the full picture. For that, we are going to have to talk more about coping strategies employed by both genders, as well as a conversation on hormones and its role in ADHD. We will cover this in the coming chapters, as well as a focus on specific life-events such as puberty, supporting your daughter/foster-child, and exactly how is ADHD experienced by girls (as distinct from that experienced by boys).

As I always do point out to my clients, I will say that the information and support I provide to individuals with ADHD is from the perspective of a life coach specialising in ADHD, and if they would like a formal diagnosis of ADHD, then this must be pursued through the appropriate medical and clinical channels.

What this book covers

In this introductory guide to ADHD in girls, we will cover the signs and symptoms of ADHD in girls, how ADHD is affected by adolescence and puberty, and also the way in which ADHD differs in boys and girls. Lastly, we cover how to provide support to your child/student given the particular ways in which ADHD is experienced in girls. This introductory guide is aimed as a primer to the subject, and I have referenced research papers/other websites throughout this book. The key thing to remember is that ADHD is a real developmental disorder experienced by girls and women, and the way in which it is experienced differs from boys. It is important to validate the experiences of girls, as all to often their signs and symptoms are ignored for a variety of reasons. This book is part of the effort to redress the balance and provide the much needed support to girls suffering from ADHD.

Signs and Symptoms in Girls

I t might be strange for people to see a section and chapter on signs and symptoms of ADHD in girls, however research has shown that ADHD remains largely misunderstood by the general public[4]. This is all the more pertinent as females are more likely to have the attention deficit subtype of ADHD compared to the hyperactivity subtype. Understanding the ways in which ADHD manifests itself in girls is a helpful exercise, particularly as our understanding of the symptoms of ADHD in females is growing on an almost daily basis.

In the below section I have listed three tell-tale signs that may be due to undiagnosed ADHD in girls. Of course, presence of one or more of these symptoms doesn't mean your child/student definitively has ADHD, it's just that you can potentially explore the option that it may be the case (and further exploration and signs and symptoms come later in this book).

1. **Compensatory techniques used for inattention**

---

[4] https://www.annualreviews.org/doi/10.1146/annurev-clinpsy-050817-084917

For many girls with ADHD it is paying attention to what is happening right at that moment in time, that is their biggest challenge. They can get distracted by the internal musings of their mind, or perhaps even external events that are taking place. For example, if a girl in sitting in a classroom, then the mere presence of a bird outside the classroom window may divert her attention away from something that is happening within the class, such as the teacher giving the class an important piece of information about an upcoming assignment.

To compensate for this inattention, a girl with ADHD may employ the strategy of *hyperfocus*. This basically means that the girl focuses intensely on something that she is good at/enjoys (or both). Sometimes so much effort and attention is paid to these interests that parents or educators may dismiss outright the possibility of any ADHD (as it doesn't fit the 'typical' signs). However, this *hyperfocus* could be used as a coping mechanism by a girl to keep herself entertained when she find something particularly boring. The challenge however, is that it may also be the case that this *hyperfocus* is very difficult for the girl to control.

2. A tomboy or hyperactive?

Perhaps the most famous symptom of ADHD is its hyperactivity, however if a girl is hyperactive then it may be the case that she is called a tomboy just because she enjoys the great outdoors and the physical activity that that brings. Another reason why a girl's hyperactivity may be masked is because of the discrete ways in which girls the hyperactivity is displayed. For example, constant motion due to a girl's ADHD may be presented through constantly scribbling and doodling, or perhaps fidgeting around in her chair.

3. Lack of impulse control

The final symptom that I am going to talk about from a female perspective is the symptom of impulsivity. An impulsive girl could be extremely talkative and loquacious, constantly talking and interrupting others – perhaps even shifting conversations midway whilst talking to somebody. She might even inappropriately blurt out words without really thinking about the way those words land on others, and the impact that those words can have. The other dimension of a lack of impulse control is in being overly sensitive. Some girls with ADHD are prone to being easily excitable and some may regard even over emotional.

Look out for the internal symptoms

It was a review of studies published in 2014[5] that suggested girls and women with ADHD are much more likely to have an internal symptom that is not visible to others. It is for this reason that we would ask that you particularly look out for symptoms that are not external, but rather, internal and could be linked to the distractibility of the mind and inattentiveness. The studies also found that for a number of reasons, girls may develop better coping strategies in comparison with boys that have ADHD, and as a result the true extent of ADHD in girls is underdiagnosed.

Furthermore if your daughter/student has a few of the below

---

[5]   https://www.ncbi.nlm.nih.gov/pmc/articles/PMC4195638/

signs and symptoms a further discussion with a professional may be warranted:

- She appears to be withdrawn, on a regular basis
- She is prone to crying easily
- She finds it difficult to remain focused on the subject in hand, and to complement this, she is easily distracted
- She spends a significant proportion of her time daydreaming and is often lost in her own thoughts
- She has lost motivation, and doesn't appear to be trying hard academically/socially
- She is often messy and disorganised (both in the physical space she maintains – i.e. her bedroom, and in her appearance)
- She is highly sensitive to emotions, fabrics and noise
- She is loquacious (always has lots to say, but isn't necessarily that good at listening)
- She is forgetful
- She is overly emotional and has exaggerated responses
- She seemingly makes lots of 'not thought out' mistakes
- She has bad time management
- she can get upset very easily
- she often shifts her attention and focus from one activity to another
- she constantly interrupts others
- It can seem like she is taking time to process thoughts and can seem like she is not really hearing you

ADHD and Puberty

W e all know that adolescence can be a particularly testing time. For those who also suffer from ADHD, this period in one's life can be particularly difficult. We know from research that children who suffer from ADHD have lower emotional maturity levels compared with their peers, that means that as soon as puberty kicks in for these girls and boys they have to deal with it with much lower emotional maturity levels.

New research is beginning to show that the flood of hormonal changes that puberty brings with it can wreak havoc in the lives of girls with ADHD[6]. It is a time when many who previously had undetected ADHD get diagnosed. If you have a daughter/student with ADHD you might be wondering as to how these hormonal changes will interact with her ADHD[7]. In this chapter I will cover some of the key things to look out for in the interplay between hormonal changes caused by puberty and a child's ADHD.

---

[6] http://www.psychiatrist.com/pcc/article/pages/route.aspx?u=/pcc/article/-pages/2014/v16n03/13r01596.aspx

[7] This is a good summary of the role of oestrogen in ADHD

Many changes take place in a girl's life as she begins that transition from being a child into an adult. The body grows and develops both physically as well as sexually, and alongside these changes there are a range of social, biological and mental changes that take place too. Often these changes are confusing enough to the child, without the added complication of ADHD, however under normal circumstances these changes are entirely normal. It is only when a child has ADHD, that these hormonal changes can cause behavioural challenges for them. For example, some girls with ADHD can become hyper irritable during this period and may even have feelings of panic, acute anxiety and very noticeable mood swings.

Self-esteem in particular may take a knock as negative thoughts about themselves can begin to develop. This display of internalised symptoms is entirely in line with the way in which girls suffer from an internalised variant of ADHD. The difficulties usually associated with ADHD such as the inability to focus , being prone to distraction and not having good organisation skills, can noticeably increase during puberty, and leave girls feeling completely overwhelmed.

Other research found that girls with ADHD in the early teens tended to have more academic problems and they also had earlier signs of substance -related issues and higher rates of depression[8]. There are also some indicative studies that has shown that *oestrogen* may alter a woman's response to ADHD medication, and that this effect is also diminished in the presence of *progesterone.*

---

[8] https://www.additudemag.com/puberty-and-adhd-symptoms-teens/

If you're finding that your child's ADHD symptoms worsen during her pre menstrual cycle, you could encourage her to complete any assignment due ahead of time, especially if there is a big test due during her menstrual cycle. It is also perhaps a good idea to keep a journal documenting how her ADHD symptoms are exacerbated by hormonal fluctuations. This will help you plan well for any additional challenges that you may have, as well as the individualised areas that she struggles with in particular.

As this book is meant to be an introduction to the subject I will reference some further reading for those of you who wish to delve down deeper into the subject. I particularly recommend a paper written by Patricia Quinn and Manisha Madhoo[9], both of whom are Medical Doctors and wrote a paper on clinical presentation of ADHD in women and girls and the factors that influence a proper diagnosis and treatment.

It is important to mention here that the average age of diagnosis for women with ADHD who haven't been diagnosed as children, is approximately 37 *years old.* Before that time there is often a misdiagnosis where ADHD is either misunderstood as either a mood disorder or an anxiety disorder. The hormonal challenges and symptoms of ADHD being intensified by the premenstrual cycle continue to exist during adulthood as well, so in many ways this is a lifelong adjustment that would need to be made. You can read a bit more about this in my book on ADHD and

---

[9] https://www.researchgate.net/publication/266946231_A_Review_of_Attention-DeficitHyperactivity_Disorder_in_Women_and_Girls

Women.

How is ADHD different in Girls

In the past decade or so, knowledge and public understanding of ADHD has increased. Primarily it is still understood as a disorder that mainly affects boys. Research over the past 5 to 6 years has begun to develop a deeper understanding of the prevalence of ADHD in girls and women as well as trying to understand how and whether signs and symptoms of ADHD differ in girls compared with boys[10].

A summary of this research over the past few years allows us to make a few outline comments. We can say almost definitively that girls don't usually display symptoms that are typical of ADHD behaviour (as understood by the general public), and in fact the symptoms may not be as recognisable in girls as they are in boys. Girls with ADHD display more internalised aspects of the disorder and tend to suffer from the inattentive subtype of ADHD whereas boys struggle mainly with the hyperactive tendencies of ADHD[11].

---

[10] https://bmcpsychiatry.biomedcentral.com/articles/10.1186/s12888-020-02707-9

[11] https://childmind.org/article/how-to-help-girls-with-adhd

Hyperactive behaviour can be easier to identify in the classroom because the child isn't able to sit in one place and also because she/he can behave in an impulsive manner. Inattentive behaviour, is, by its very definition, less discernible. The child isn't likely to be disruptive in school but will be forgetful and feel to meet assignment deadlines or perhaps even just seem to be in a world of their own and daydreaming. This is sometimes mistaken for procrastination, laziness or even a special educational need. This can cause issues in the identification of ADHD in girls, and as a result ADHD can be under reported and under diagnosed in females as compared with males. Wider understanding of the various subtypes of ADHD is required by parents, educators and administrators to be able to provide the most adequate support for young girls with the neurodevelopmental disorder.

Girls often have some of the following symptoms

- Feeling withdrawn
- Suffering from low self-esteem and being prone to anxiety
- Finding it difficult to achieve academically at the level that they ought to be
- The tendency to daydream and being inattentive
- Having trouble focusing
- Partaking in a verbal are such as name-calling or teasing
- It seeming that they are not listening

The power of personal stories

On the website childmind.org, Rae Jacobson has written an

excellent article entitled how girls with ADHD are different[12]. In it she talks about her own personal story of being prone to lateness and losing things as a child. it's a very touching account of ADHD and I highly recommend reading it.

I often find that personal accounts are incredibly helpful for the individual I'm coaching and if your daughter/student is struggling with her ADHD symptoms then sharing stories such as these will be incredibly powerful in them feeling supported with their ADHD. I would encourage you to read the article above as well as perhaps even encouraging your daughter/student to write down their own story so that it, in turn, can be shared with others.

---

[12] https://childmind.org/article/how-girls-with-adhd-are-different/

Supporting your child

N ow that we have covered some of the key signs and symptoms of ADHD in girls, this section covers what we can do to help girls with ADHD.

Whilst supporting children with ADHD through medication and other adjustments in the school and home environments is beneficial, girls face a particular set of challenges and parents/educators need an approach that can tackle these particular challenges.

Most girls with ADHD suffer from the inattentive subtype, and this means that their symptoms are largely hidden. As a result, their ADHD often goes unnoticed and unacknowledged. Furthermore instead of being diagnosed with ADHD, girls can often face criticism from teachers, peers and even their parents (for these very symptoms), and this can have a knock-on effect on their self esteem.

The more you as a parent or teacher can educate yourself and those around you regarding this complex and frustrating disorder, the more support you be able to provide for your daughter/student, and you will be able to be a stand and advocate for her in the face of potential stigma and misunderstanding.

For example, some parents, when asked about the most difficult aspect of dealing with their child's ADHD, talked about it being an invisible disorder and how they had never heard of girls having ADHD. Because it was so subtle, it seemed like their children were doing fine at school and with their friendship networks, but in actual fact they were struggling academically and socially.

Forming a strong support network with other parents of children who have ADHD is critically important. This is because the parent without ADHD will at times not fully understand the disorder, and will frequently misunderstand signs and symptoms of ADHD (e.g. the inattentiveness and forgetfulness). This is why clinical psychologists who specialise in ADHD suggest that parents with ADHD daughters spent time discussing their children with other parents who have similar struggles. Hearing the similarities in the stories can help to build the resilience of parents, as well as helping them create strategies in order to help them understand the disorder better, and in creating strategies for supporting their daughters as well.

An area that is often overlooked is helping girls with ADHD in their friendship networks. Girls with ADHD sometimes struggle to *create and keep friendship* networks, especially as the complexities of a girl's social environment are already overwhelming during the teenage years. As soon as you add in a neurodevelopmental disorder such as ADHD then you can quickly appreciate the challenges and pitfalls that can *and do* occur.

One suggestion in this regard is to help girls with ADHD find social outlets that they feel very comfortable within, as well as to find out their strengths, and to let them play to these strengths accordingly. For example, f it is the case that your daughter struggles in a particular social environment then find settings that encourage and accept participation from a wider variety of people. These could be gatherings that are either supervised, and gatherings that value kindness and treating others with respect.

It is very important to encourage girls with ADHD to become involved in clubs and activities that focus on their interests. Examples include book groups, art classes, and other topic based discussion groups. This will help her learn to feel comfortable, confident and safe in a setting with other young people. If it is the case that your daughter/student also has symptoms of the hyperactive subtype of ADHD, such as impulsivity, then perhaps select social settings where she can release energy such as a sports activity or a theatre group.

Normalising the experiences a girl with ADHD suffers from, and talking about those concerns as being legitimate issues that need to be talked about, is also very important in order for them not to feel alienated. One strategy may be buying and reading books about 'ADHD in girls/women' and to discuss sections within the book that either piqued her interest or were triggering in one way or another. I believe there are a number of good books written about this subject, that are available at all major book retailers. (if you wait to listen to the bonus section at the end of this book, I have included how you can access a free audiobook on ADHD and women offered by Mental Health Publishing).

Environmental scaffolding is another strategy that could be employed to support a girl with ADHD. This works through creating situations that increase the girl's self-esteem, confidence, and abilities, whilst at the same time offers support in the areas where they feel less confident. As an example, girls with hyperactivity could benefit from the creation of a study club, in case studying alone by oneself would make studying next to impossible, this way she would be at ease in a social atmosphere, and constructive use would be made of her skill set in order to fulfil the goal of doing well academically and studying. On the contrary, girls who may be more introverted that struggle with distractions, may fare better in an environment that is quiet, relaxing and distraction free. Please note that some people struggle more with visual stimuli and others with aural stimuli, and it would be a good idea to find out which types of distractions are are particularly bad for the girl in question.

A lot of the research shows that girls with ADHD suffer from low self esteem. Finding ways of remedying this and dealing with this is also crucial in supporting her with her ADHD. This problem of low self esteem can be particularly problematic for those who have been undiagnosed. The reason low self esteem is such a problem is because of the constant "failures" encountered in the home or school setting. For example, in forgetting homework for the umpteenth time, or forgetting to wash the dishes at home the umpteenth time, the young person can be labelled as lazy, forgetful etc, but an ill-informed parent or educator.

Not only are the academic difficulties faced by girls with ADHD particularly acute, the emotional challenges suffered can be equally or more severe than these academic difficulties. Girls with ADHD have higher rate of suicide attempts, as well as substance abuse and self-harm incidences. This unfortunate fact is also known from our research on ADHD affecting adults. There are higher rates of comorbidities (particularly depression and anxiety) in people with ADHD.

Focusing on the strength that they possess is a key way to regaining that self esteem, and to build up a more positive self image. Find what works, and what they're good at, and then scaffold their lives with support so that those interests can flourish and become a major focus and central point in their life.

Finally, talking about ADHD - the good, the bad, and the ugly, can be incredibly liberating. Girls with ADHD tend to compensate for their difficulties whilst being too embarrassed to ask for support. This is why talking as much as you can, about the things that you - as an adult/educator/mentor/parent - might need help with, can encourage them to become accustomed to get comfortable with asking for help themselves, in the areas that they need it in. This can take some time, and will require practice for her to find the strength to be able to articulate her needs, especially as we all too often live in a world where our needs are not properly articulated, and in fact, we are afraid to do so.

A good book in this regard, is Stephen Cory's classic, 'The Seven Habits of Highly Successful People'. In the book, Stephen highlights the different levels of engagement a human has with other humans. The book talks about an individual's journey moving from dependence through to independence but then finally arriving at the apex, which is not independence but rather *interdependence.* This is where humans recognise that we need help and support from each other, and it is only in this state that we truly actualise our abilities, capabilities and true potential. As the saying famously goes, "*no man (or woman!) is an island.*"

Conclusion

All the research suggest that it is clear that ADHD is experienced very differently by girls and young women. Ground breaking work has taken place over the last decade on a number of areas, including the role of hormones in the exacerbation of the signs and symptoms of ADHD in girls, as well as the identification of various subtypes of ADHD (with girls being significantly more likely to have the inattentive subtype). There is a lot more work to do in order to be able to ensure that every young girls who suffers from ADHD has the appropriate level of support from her school and home environments.

In this book we started off looking at the signs and symptoms of ADHD within girls in contradistinction with boys, trying to identify the key areas they struggle with. I have pointed out three key areas here: firstly, the fact that girls largely suffer from the inattentive sub variant of ADHD means that the condition is largely invisible and as such there needs to be a greater understanding of the condition in general. Secondly, the invisibility of the condition means that a girls self-esteem can take a serious knock, and additional support for parents, schools and the girls with ADHD is required. These mental health issues can quickly morph into something much bigger, within a short space of time, and so this is an issue that needs tackling sensitivity but assuredly. Thirdly, I covered some of the things to look out for in your child, student etc, which may act as tell tale signs of ADHD.

In ADHD and puberty, we looked at some specific female only issues such as the menstrual cycle and how the onset of this within puberty and adolescence for girls, is an area that needs special attention when it comes to supporting a girl with ADHD. We talked about the role of oestrogen in ADHD, and how hormones can and do affect the way in which ADHD symptoms are experienced by women. All is not lost however, there is much more knowledge about these factors and I have highlighted some ways in which you can help support your daughter/student at this time.

Next we looked a little more in depth at the difference between ADHD in boys and girls, and listed out some of the specific ways in which girls can be challenged by ADHD. We looked at how personal accounts of ADHD can be extremely powerful, and a suggestion to find these personal accounts as well as perhaps starting your own. These days blogging can be done entirely for free via a wordpress blog, and you can meet like minded people through the process.

Finally we looked at some specific strategies and techniques for supporting your daughter/student with their ADHD. We pointed out that having support for yourself is also very important and to not neglect yourself in that process and we looked at some of the ways in which to boost your child's self esteem, and how you can engineer an environment within with your child/student can thrive (supporting them with their friendship networks, without seeming too over bearing is one area I would definitely invest in).

The most important thing to point out is that you are already on that journey now so you don't have to feel alone in your quest to find out more about ADHD. You can connect with us here at Mental Health Publishing via Facebook, Twitter and Pinterest. We would love to hear from you and you can also find more resources on our website mentalhealthpublishing.com. If you have found some of these strategies useful and helpful then please leave us a helpful review, we would really appreciate it.

An audiobook bonus for readers

As you have come this far in your journey to find out more about ADHD in girls, would you like to receive a free Audiobook on ADHD and women as a thank you from us here at Mental Health Publishing?

If you would, then please visit navigate to mentalhealthpublishing.com forward slash freeadhdwomenbook. Here, you can listen to a sample of the audiobook (narrated by One Voice awards nominee, Nikki Delgado), as well as sign up to our newsletter. Once you have given your email address you will be redirected to a page with the entire Audiobook (retailing for $2.99 on most international retailers).

A humble request

This is just a humble request for a review if you have learnt anything about ADHD and girls through this short guide, or found some of the tips and strategies helpful. Reviews help us to be able to build up an appreciation of the kind of content that was particularly useful to our readers, and allows us to replicate that in our other upcoming publications.

You can also connect with us via our website on mentalhealth-publishing.com

Related Books

If you enjoyed this short book then you may enjoy the following titles by the same author.

ADHD and Women

Get Organised With ADHD

Managing Relationships with ADHD